P9-EET-866

We Need Communications Workers

by Brienna Rossiter

FOCUS READERS

PIONEER

www.focusreaders.com

Focus Readers is distributed by North Star Editions:
sales@northstareditions.com | 888-417-0195

Produced for Focus Readers by Red Line Editorial.

Photographs ©: Shutterstock Images, cover, 1, 4, 7, 8, 11 (top), 11 (bottom), 12, 15, 18, 21; iStockphoto, 17

Library of Congress Cataloging-in-Publication Data
Library of Congress Cataloging-in-Publication Data is available on the Library of Congress website.

ISBN
978-1-63739-028-3 (hardcover)
978-1-63739-082-5 (paperback)
978-1-63739-189-1 (ebook pdf)
978-1-63739-136-5 (hosted ebook)

Printed in the United States of America
Mankato, MN
012022

About the Author

Brienna Rossiter is a writer and editor who lives in Minnesota.

Table of Contents

Chapter 1

Communications

People **communicate** in many ways. They talk on phones. They send messages. They see posts online. They video chat, too. Communications workers help make all these things possible.

Some workers help share information. For example, reporters tell people the news. Other workers fix the systems people use. They keep websites and **devices** working well.

Chapter 2

Helping Users

Many workers help people use the internet and phones. They often work for phone or internet companies. Some workers do repairs. They fix phone lines or **cell towers**.

Other workers help users solve problems. They may answer emails or phone calls. Or they may travel to people's homes. They make sure the internet and phones are working.

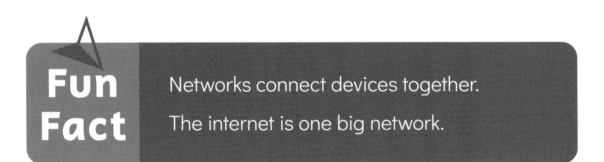

Fun Fact
Networks connect devices together. The internet is one big network.

Supporting Systems

The internet uses many devices to send information. Some workers fix these devices. Others plan how devices work together. They find the best way to send information.

13

Many workers help keep websites running. They may write **code**. Code tells what a website will look like or do. Some people write new code. Others make updates. They find and fix problems.

Software

Phones and computers run **software**. Many workers help to make this software. Some plan what it will do. They keep making newer, better versions. They fix problems. And they make software easier for people to use. Workers write code to make these plans happen. They test the code, too.

Chapter 4

Storing Data

People and companies use lots of information. **Databases** and data centers help store this information. Workers help build them and keep them running smoothly.

Workers also keep information safe. They work to stop **hacks**. And they plan what to do if a system breaks. They make sure the information doesn't get lost or stolen.

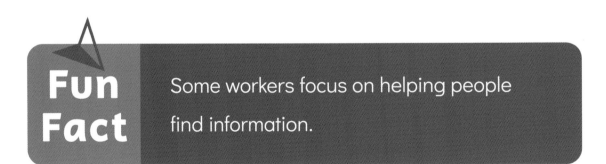

Fun Fact Some workers focus on helping people find information.

FOCUS ON
Communications Workers

Write your answers on a separate piece of paper.

1. Write a sentence telling one thing that communications workers help people do.

2. Do you prefer using phones or computers to communicate? Why?

3. What do reporters do?
   - A. build cell towers
   - B. tell people the news
   - C. fix people's devices

4. What is an example of a hack?
   - A. Someone steals another person's information.
   - B. Someone writes new software.
   - C. Someone works at a data center.

Answer key on page 24.

Glossary

cell towers
Tall towers that send and receive the signals used by phones.

code
Instructions that tell a computer or device what to do.

communicate
To share ideas or news with another person.

databases
Systems that store and sort large amounts of information.

devices
Phones, tablets, or other objects that are made to do certain tasks.

hacks
Times when people get information or control computers in ways that break the law.

software
Sets of code that run on a device to tell it how to do certain jobs.

To Learn More

BOOKS

Ayarbe, Heidi. *Electricians on the Job*. Mankato, MN: The Child's World, 2020.

Gagne, Tammy. *Smartphones*. Minneapolis: Abdo Publishing, 2019.

NOTE TO EDUCATORS

Visit **www.focusreaders.com** to find lesson plans, activities, links, and other resources related to this title.

Index

Answer Key: 1. Answers will vary; **2.** Answers will vary; **3.** B; **4.** A